MUSIC

FOR

SIGHT

SINGING

PRENTICE-HALL INTERNATIONAL, INC., *London*

PRENTICE-HALL OF AUSTRALIA, PTY. LTD., *Sydney*

PRENTICE-HALL OF CANADA, LTD., *Toronto*

PRENTICE-HALL OF INDIA (PRIVATE) Ltd., *New Delhi*

PRENTICE-HALL OF JAPAN, INC., *Tokyo*

MUSIC

FOR

SIGHT

SINGING

second edition

Robert W. Ottman
Professor of Music
North Texas State University

Prentice-Hall, Inc., Englewood Cliffs, New Jersey

Library of Congress Catalog Card Number : 67-11101

Printed in the United States of America.

Preface

To become successful in sight singing, one must have at his disposal a considerable amount of singable and musical material. This material should be graded so that he will be able to study one problem at a time and to progress steadily from the easiest material to the most complex. The music in this collection has been compiled with both these aims in mind. It has been drawn from the works of reputable composers and from a wide range of the world's folk music. None of the material has been written expressly for sight singing.

This book subscribes to no particular method of learning music theory. Therefore it can be used successfully in conjunction with almost any book on theory. The objective is not to present a course in music theory but rather to furnish sight-singing material to be used in conjunction with the study of theory. Chapter introductions are limited to descriptions of the organization of each chapter and occasional suggested aids to the singer.

There are two technical factors in the construction of any melody: rhythm and melody. For this reason, the melodies in this volume are graded according to both rhythmic and melodic difficulty. Each chapter introduces a new problem in relation to one or the other factor but not to both simultaneously.

The three major sections of the book control the rhythmic development, whereas each chapter within the sections develops skill in reading intervals. The study of intervals begins with melodies containing only scale passages and skips in the tonic triad. (Melodies composed exclusively of scale-wise passages are not included because they are almost nonexistent in folk or composed music, except in ecclesiastical chants.) In this context the skips are easy to sing. Instruction progresses slowly to the V and IV triads followed by a study of the same intervals in more difficult contexts.

Because the material is so minutely graded and each chapter introduces only one specific problem, the order of chapters may be shifted to suit almost any method of learning theory. The arrangement of material in this book has been made primarily to facilitate reference to any particular melodic or rhythmic problem.

All the music is within easy singing range. The highest note for most melodies is E♭ or lower, although there is an occasional E or F. Higher notes occur in the upper parts of ensemble music, but in these cases there is always a lower part in a range suitable for lower voices.

Many examples of rounds, canons, music in two parts, and studies in the important C clefs are integrated with the other material.

Because of the harmonic presentation of intervals, the contents of Parts I and II are limited almost exclusively to music of the eighteenth and nineteenth centuries in addition to folk music of a similar nature. In Part III the range of styles is considerably broadened for experience in singing music from the thirteenth-century troubadours to the present time.

Although the revised edition maintains the format and concepts of the original edition, many improvements within individual chapters have been made. The opening chapters have been enlarged and more carefully graded to make easier the students' beginning efforts. More emphasis has been placed on the use of the minor mode and the bass clef. Many melodies have been replaced by others that demonstrate the technical problem more efficiently and musically. More two-part examples are included, and the total number of melodies exceeds that of the original edition.

Robert W. Ottman

I

THE

BEAT

AND

ITS

DIVISION

Contents

Rhythm

Rhythm

Simple and Compound Time

a. *diatonic intervals*

b. *chromatic tones not implying modulation*

14

Melody

No New Material

Rhythm

Syncopation

a. *syncopation in the divided beat only, combined with rhythmic problems in the subdivided beat*

b. *syncopation within the subdivision of the beat*

15

Melody

Modulation to Closely Related Keys

Rhythm

Simple and Compound Time

MORE DIFFICULT MELODIC AND RHYTHMIC PROBLEMS

16

Review of Parts I and II∼Melodies More Difficult but Within the Melodic and Rhythmic Limitations of Parts I and II

MUSIC

FOR

SIGHT

SINGING

1

Melody

step-wise movement plus
intervals in the tonic (I) triad

Rhythm

simple time (meter) — the beat
and its division into two parts

The melodies of this chapter contain a wide variety of intervals. The problem of singing these intervals is made easy because they are all readily recognizable parts of the tonic triad. In E♭ major, for example, these intervals are:

* M=major, m=minor, P=perfect.

Before singing, the following plan of preparation is recommended:

1. Determine the key.
2. Spell the tonic triad.
3. Locate the tonic triad on the staff.
4. Scan the melody for examples of intervals in the tonic triad.
5. Sing the tonic triad.

Try this procedure on the following melody:

3

Note that : 1. The key is E♭ major.
2. The tonic triad is spelled E♭ G B♭.
3. The tonic triad is located on the first, second, and third lines. Also locate higher and lower tones of the triad on the staff.

1   3   5   1   5

4. Find intervals that are members of this triad :

etc.

1   3   5   5   1   5   3   5
meas. 1 — 2   ‖ meas. 4 — 6   ‖

Melodies in minor keys, beginning with melody 45, can be studied in the same way :

5   1   3   1   1   3   5   5   3   1

All melodies are in simple time using no note value smaller than the beat note and its division into two parts (background of two) :

♩ = 1 beat

1   2   3   1   (2)   (3)   1   (2)   3   1   (2)   ‿

1   2   3   1   (2)   3   1   (2)   3

Illustrations of simple time using beat notes other than the quarter note will be found, for example :

♩ = 1 beat

1   2   1   2   1   (2)   1   (2)

4

a. Major keys; treble clef; time signatures $\frac{2}{4}$, $\frac{3}{4}$, and $\frac{4}{4}$; undotted notes; intervals of the third, fourth, fifth, and octave in the tonic triad:

6

Canon for 4 voices — England

Canon for 3 voices — P. Hayes (18th century)

Canon for 3 voices — Caldara (1670–1736)

FC6DA

Canon for 3 voices — England

b. Dotted notes:

Andante — Tennessee

Allegretto — Germany

8

10

d. Interval of the sixth:

30 Allegro   United States

31 Andante   Pomerania

32 Tempo giusto   Hungary (Bartók)

33 Allegro   Mexico

11

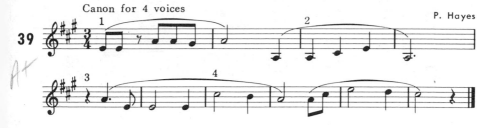

Canon for 4 voices   P. Hayes

39

e. The ♩ and ♪ as beat units :

Andante   Slovakia

40

mf

Adagio   Germany

41

p

Rousseau, Lorsque Venus pour
                                                                un berger

Andante

42

mp

p

Allegretto   Germany (Brahms)
43

Allegro   England
44

f. Minor keys :

Andante   Hungary
45

Andante   Sweden
46

Lightly   Germany
47

14

Gracefully and lively   Germany (Brahms)

48

Canon for 4 voices   Haydn

49

Allegretto   Germany (Brahms)

50

Moderato   Slovakia

51

Lento   Finland

52

53 Canon for 4 voices
England
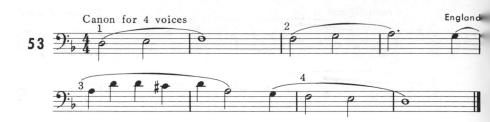

54 Slow
Germany

55 Moderato
Slovakia

56 Andante
Germany

16

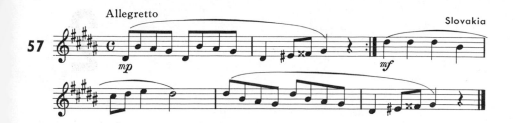

2

Melody

step-wise movement plus
intervals in the tonic triad

Rhythm

compound time — the beat
and its division into three parts

There are no new melodic problems in this chapter. All the melodies are in compound time using the beat value:

with the beat divided into three parts (background of three):

Examples of compound meter using various beat notes will be found, for example:

a. *Major keys*:

62 Allegro vivo

63 Rather slow — France

64 Moderato — Missouri

65 Allegro — France

20

71 Moderato England

72 Allegretto France

73 Allegretto Indiana

b. Minor keys :

74 Allegretto Wales

22

23

80

Allegro

England

3

Melody

intervals in the V triad

Rhythm

simple time

The same procedure outlined in Chapter 1 can be used with equal effectiveness here. After determining the key and the spelling and placing of the tonic triad, do the same with the dominant (V) triad. Then scan the melody for examples of the use of the dominant triad.

Note that: 1. The key is D major.
2. The tonic triad is spelled D F♯ A.
3. The dominant triad is spelled A C♯ E.
4. An example of the dominant triad is found in measures 5-6:

Section *d* of this chapter introduces the dominant seventh (V⁷) chord. The addition of the seventh above the V triad creates several new interval possibilities:

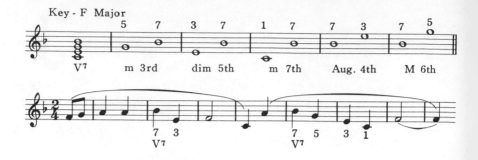

Key - F Major

a. *Intervals of the third in the V triad:*

Moderato   Germany

81

f   2nd time *p*

Moderato   Germany

82

Andantino   Italy

83

84 Allegro — Germany (Brahms)

85 Allegretto — Louisiana

Canon for 4 voices — Germany

86

87 Schnell — England

88 Moderato — Germany

Mozart, *The Abduction from the Seraglio, K. 384*

b. *Intervals of fourths and fifths in the V triad:*

96   Allegro   France

97   Vif   Louisiana

accel. e cresc.

98   Canon for 2 voices   Germany

99   Canon for 2 voices   Wachsmann (1791–1853)

30

100 Ziemlich schnell — Schubert, *Erstarrung*, Op. 89, No. 4

101 Andante — Béranger, *Ce Jour-là*

102 Lebhaft — Germany (Brahms)

103 Allegro — Germany (Brahms)

104   Andante   Germany

c. *Interval of the sixth in the V triad:*

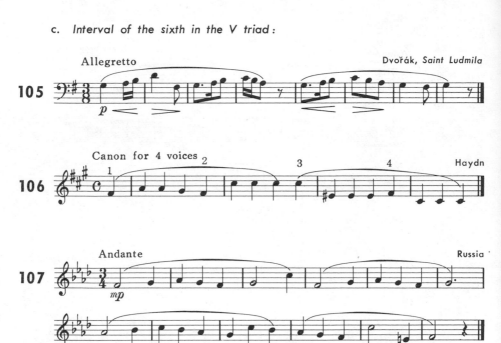

105   Allegretto   Dvořák, *Saint Ludmila*

106   Canon for 4 voices   Haydn

107   Andante   Russia

108   Moderato   Negro Spiritual

d. Intervals in the V⁷ chord:

33

34

D.C.

118

Andante
Ohio
Fine
f

D.C.
mp

119 Canon for 4 voices
Hauptmann

120 Canon for 3 voices
Caldara
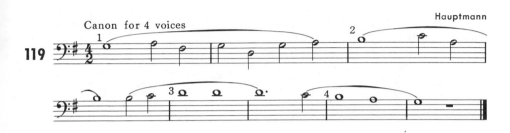

121 Canon for 4 voices
Germany

125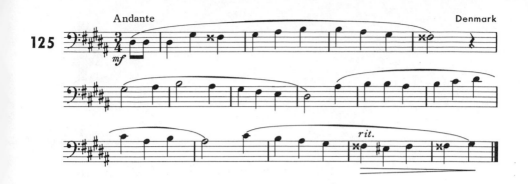

4

Melody
intervals in the V and V⁷ chords

Rhythm
compound time

The melodic problems are the same as those in the preceding chapter. The rhythmic problems are the same as those in Chapter 2, with the exceptions of melodies 142-145. Each of these melodies has a time signature of $\frac{3}{4}$ or $\frac{3}{8}$, with a very fast tempo indication. The effect is that of compound time, one beat per measure, for example, $\frac{3}{8}$: $\downarrow\cdot$ =1 beat, each, with a background of ♪♪♪ .

132 Moderato   England

133 Presto   Wolf-Ferrari, *The Jewels of the Madonna*

134 Andantino   Massenet, *Les Femmes de Magdala*

135 Allegretto   Maine

tempo

140 Lento

France

p

rit. - - - - - - - - - - a

141 Allegro

Massenet, Première Danse

p

p

142 Fast (♩· = 1 beat)

Germany

f

Fine *mf*

mf

D.C. al Fine

143 Allegro (♩.=1 beat)   Mozart, Divertimento No. 2, K. 131

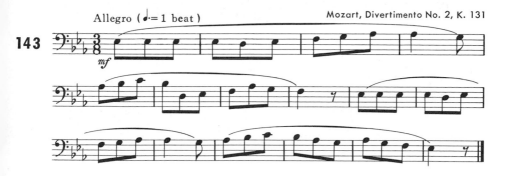

mf

144 Allegro (♩.=1 beat)   Germany (Brahms)

p

f

rit. - - - - - - - - - - - - - - - - a

tempo

145 Canon for 3 voices (♩.=1 beat)   Anonymous

5

The C Clefs

the alto and tenor clefs

The clef sign 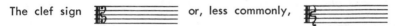 or, less commonly, indicates the location of middle C on the staff. When found on the third line of the staff, the C clef is known as the "alto clef"; when found on the fourth line, it is known as the "tenor clef."

Alto clef   *Tenor clef*

The alto clef is commonly used by the viola, and the tenor clef is used by the cello and trombone.

The music of this chapter involves a review of the problems of the previous chapters. Each example is in either the alto or tenor clef. Further study in C-clef sight singing can be done by means of clef transposition of any melody in the treble or bass clef.

To illustrate, let us take melody 14 from Chapter 1, which begins as follows:

First, observe that the tonic note of the key is on the second line. Next, cover the treble clef sign and the key signature; visualize in its place an alto clef. When using the alto clef, you will find that the second line on the staff is A; therefore, in the alto clef, this melody will be in the key of A major. Then, by visualizing an alto clef and a key signature of three sharps, one can sing the melody in the key of A major (or, with four flats, in the key of A♭ major).

The same procedure can be used for the tenor clef. Because the second line in the tenor clef is F, the melody can be sung in the key of F major (or F♯ major).

When the melody does not start on the tonic, be sure to find the tonic note of the original melody and work from that note when transposing. For example, in melody 4 in Chapter 1:

Two other C clefs and one F clef, which are not used in printed music today, can be utilized for transposition. They are:

Soprano clef

Mezzo soprano clef

Baritone clef

These three plus the treble, bass, alto, and tenor clefs comprise a group of seven clefs by which any pitch name can be transposed to any other pitch name. Adding appropriate accidentals will give any major or minor key signature.

C D E F G A B

146 Andane — England

147 Allegretto — England

148 Canon for 4 voices — Webbe (c. 1680)

149 Lively — Netherlands

1.   2.

150 Andante — Poland

156 Allegro

Schubert, *Der Musensohn*, Op. 92, No. 1

157 Allegretto

France

158 Moderato

Germany

159 Allegretto

England

49

160 Canon for 4 voices   England

161 Animé   France

162 Lively   Germany

163 Canon for 4 voices   England

164 Allegro   Germany

50

165 Andantino — Germany

166 Canon for 4 voices — Praetorius

167 England

168 Moderato — Moniot D'Arras (13th century), Ce fut en mai

169

6

Melody

intervals in the IV triad

Rhythm

simple time

In the preceding chapters, all intervals commonly used in melodic construction have been studied. The I, V, and V⁷ chords contained these intervals: major third, minor third, perfect fourth, perfect fifth, diminished fifth, major sixth, minor sixth, minor seventh, the perfect octave, and the scale steps (major and minor seconds). The remaining intervals are infrequently used in melodic writing and will be noted in subsequent chapters when they occur.

Intervals used in connection with the IV triad fall into two classifications:
1. Both notes of the interval are clearly within the IV triad structure.

2. The interval appears to be in a IV triad structure when in reality there is a chord change from one note of the interval to the next.

(Study of this same problem, but concerning chords other than the IV, is continued in Chapter 8.)

With the skill gained from performing the basic intervals in the previous chapters, there should be no real difficulty in mastering these same intervals in their new contexts.

a. *Intervals of the third in the IV triad:*

74 Adagio   Westphalia

175 Moderato   Memel

176 Allegretto   Swabia

177 Allegro moderato   England

b. Other intervals in the IV triad:

58

192

Canon for 4 voices

7

Melody
intervals in the IV triad

Rhythm
compound time

The melodic problems are the same as those in the preceding chapter. The rhythmic problems are the same as those in Chapters 1 and 3.

195 Adagio — England

196 Moderato — Oklahoma

197 Modéré — France

198 Con spirito — United States*

* From *Americans and Their Songs* by Frank Luther, New York, N.Y., 22

203 Moderato   Schubert, *Der Entfernten*

8

Melody

1. intervals in triads other than I, IV, and V
2. other interval problems

Rhythm

simple and compound time

1. Occasionally, intervals are found that imply chords other than I, IV, and V. An example of this can be found in melody 205 in which the supertonic triad is outlined in the second full measure.

2. Quite often each note of the interval represents a different chord. This problem was introduced in Chapter 6. An example can be found in melody 207, measures 3 and 4. The interval of a major sixth, F down to Ab, occurs during a change from the II to the I triad.

Section b of this chapter introduces the chromatically altered tone when this altered tone does not imply a modulation. These tones may be altered non-harmonic tones or may imply the location of an altered chord.

a. *Diatonic intervals:*

206 Presto   Haydn, Symphony No. 100

207 Canon for 3 voices   Schubert

208 Allegro   France

209 Lento   Beethoven, Quartet No. 16, Op. 135

210   Andante   Germany

211   Andante con moto   Mendelssohn, *Das Schifflein,*
                                              Op. 99, No. 4

212   Andante   Campian (16th century) *Never
                                  Weather-Beaten Sail*

213   Canon for 3 voices   Mozart

66

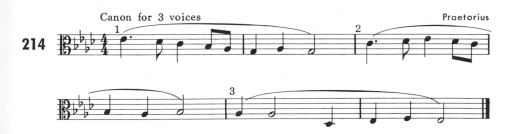

214 Canon for 3 voices — Praetorius

215 Canon for 3 voices — England

216 Canon for 4 voices — Germany

217 Canon for 3 voices — England

218 Andante sostenuto

Massenet, Chant Provençal

p *dolce*

poco rit.

219 Moderato

England

mf

220 Nicht schnell

Schumann, *Blondels Lied*, Op. 53, No. 1

p

f

Hindemith, *Let's Build a Town*

224

Mozart, *Marriage of Figaro*, K. 492

225

Andante

70

226 Allegro vivace assai Mozart, Quartet, K. 458

227 Canon for 2 duets Zelter (1758–1832)

228 Allegro Mozart, *The Magic Flute*, K. 620

b. *Chromatic tones not implying modulation:*

229 Con moto   Ireland

230 Andante   Canada

231 Allegro — Brahms, *Der Schmied*, Op. 19, No. 4

232 Animated — Brahms, *Vergebliches Ständchen*, Op. 84, No. 4

233 Moderato — Costa Rica

234 Giocoso — Virgin Islands

235 Moderato   Chopin, *Das Ringlein*

236 Langsam   Beethoven, *An die ferne Geliebte,* Op. 98

237 Canon for 3 voices   Beethoven

238 Canon for 3 voices   Purcell

74

239 Grazioso

Mendelssohn, *Der Blumenstrauss,*
Op. 47, No. 5

240 Canon for 3 voices

Beethoven

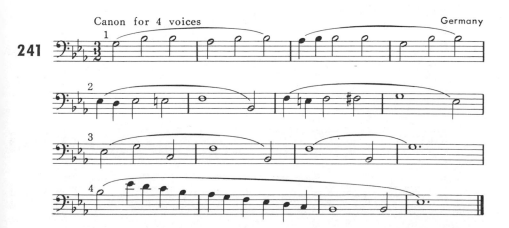

241 Canon for 4 voices

Germany

242 Allegretto Italy

* Interval of a diminished third.

243 Moderato Beethoven, *Fidelio*, Op. 72

Andante cantabile

Schumann, Quartet, Op. 47

rit.

9

Melody

no new material

Rhythm

syncopation

Syncopation occurs when the normal or expected pattern of rhythm, accent, or meter is deliberately upset. Syncopation can be created by (1) accenting a weak beat or weak part of a beat, or (2) tying a weak beat or weak part of a beat into the next strong beat or part of a beat.

248 Canon for 3 voices   Caldara

249 Andante   Negro Spiritual

mp

p

Mozart, Prague Symphony, K. 504

250 Presto

p

251 Moderato   England

252 Moderato commodo   Saint-Saëns, *Christmas Oratorio*

253 Canon for 3 voices   Caldara

254 Andante   Alabama

255 Andante con moto   Bach, Motet No. 2

256 Allegro   Spain

257 Allegro   Piccini, *Allesandro nelle Indie*

258   Fast   Arizona

259   Allegretto   Dominican Republic

260   Andante   Negro Spiritual

261

Cantabile

Arizona

Canon for 3 voices

England

262

263 Allegro   Mexico

264 Allegro   Mexico

265 Allegretto   Bohemia

Fine

266 Allegro — Bach, Brandenburg Concerto, No. 4

267 Allegro molto — Beethoven, 'Cello Sonata No. 3, Op. 69

Purcell, Dido and Aeneas

268

f Fear no dan - ger to en - sue, the

repeat

p

dim.   *p*

Fear no dan - ger to en - sue, the

he - ro loves as well as you.

Fine

he - ro loves as well as you.

Fine

p Ev - er gen - tle, ev - er smil - ing,

p

and the cares of life be - guil - ing

D.C.

D.C.

10

Melody
*modulation to closely related keys**

Rhythm
simple and compound time

Of all the possible modulations to closely related keys, the modulation to the dominant is by far the most common. For this reason a large part of this chapter is concerned with modulation to the dominant. Next in frequency of occurrence are the modulations to the relative major key and the relative minor key. Examples of these and of the other closely related modulations are found in Section *b* of this chapter.

In singing a melody with a modulation, it will be helpful to keep the following points in mind :

1. The new tonic triad should be visualized on the staff as soon as the modulation becomes apparent.

2. Some modulations may be so transient or temporary that they seem to be merely chord progressions to a half cadence, returning immediately to the key. The second phrase of melody 269 is a good example of such a temporary " modulation."

3. It is not necessary that an accidental appear in the melody line to indicate that a modulation has taken place. When the melody is harmonized, the accidental will appear in another voice (see melody 269).

---

* A closely related key is one whose tonic triad is found as a diatonic triad in the original key. The closely related keys to C major are : D minor, E minor, F major, G major, and A minor. The closely related keys to C minor are : E ♭ major, F minor, G minor, A ♭ major, and B ♭ major.

a. Modulation to the key of the dominant:

269

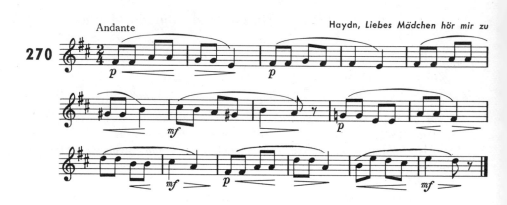

270

271

275 Andantino

Franz, Mutter, o sing mich zur Ruh!

276 Mit innigkeit

Germany

277 Allegro

Mozart, Sehnsuch nach dem
Frühlinge, K. 596

Canon for 4 voices   P. Hayes

278

Schumann, *Der Zeizig*, Op. 104,
No. 4

Munter

279

Schubert, *Der Alpenjäger*, Op. 13,
No. 3

Frisch

280

281 Allegro   Beethoven, *Busslied*, Op. 48, No. 5

282 Innig   Schumann, *Du Ring am meinem Finger*, Op. 42, No. 4

283 Allegretto vivace — Mozart, Così fan tutte, K. 588

Fine

D.C.

284 Allegro — Mozart, The Magic Flute, K. 620

Fine

Allegro con brio

285

Brahms, Trio, Op. 8

286 Vivace

Dittersdorf, *Doktor und Apotheker*

b. Modulation to other closely related keys :

287 Allegro 𝄋

Purcell, *King Arthur*

Fine

D.S. al Fine

288 Andante

Albinoni, *Ruscelletto limpidetto**

289 Andante — Gluck, *Iphigenie auf Tauris*

290 Langsam — Germany (Brahms)

Canon for 3 voices   **Purcell**

291

Andante   **Liszt, Angiolin dal biondo crin**

292

pp dolce

poco rit.   *a tempo*

poco rit.

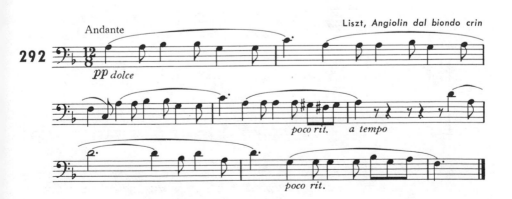

293 Canon for 2 voices

Haydn, Quartet, Op. 76, No. 2

294 Gracieusement

Rameau, *Hippolyte et Aricie*

295
Largo   Telemann, Sonatine

296
Andante con moto   Mendelssohn, *Jagdlied*, Op. 84, No. 3

297
Allegro   Mendelssohn, *Italien*, Op. 8 No. 3

298

299

300 Moderato   Rubenstein, *Volkslied*

rit.

cresc.

cresc.   dim.

cresc.

dim.   p

II

THE

BEAT

AND

ITS

SUBDIVISION

11

Melody

intervals in the I, V, V⁷, and IV chords

Rhythm

*simple time — the beat and its
subdivision into four parts*

This chapter contains no new interval problems. Section *a* includes intervals in the I and V triads as studied in Chapter 1 and Chapter 3, Sections *a*, *b*, and *c*. Section *b* includes intervals in the V⁷ chord as studied in Chapter 3, Section *d*. Section *c* includes intervals in the IV triad as studied in Chapter 6.

New in this chapter is the subdivision of the beat note into four parts; for example, in $\frac{2}{4}$ ♩ = 𝅘𝅥𝅯𝅘𝅥𝅯𝅘𝅥𝅯𝅘𝅥𝅯 ; in $\frac{2}{2}$ ♩ = ♩ ♩ ♩ ♩ ; in $\frac{3}{8}$ ♪ = 𝅘𝅥𝅯𝅘𝅥𝅯𝅘𝅥𝅯𝅘𝅥𝅯 . Several rhythmic patterns can be formed by tying various members of this four-note group:

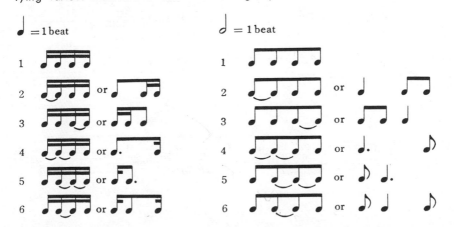

Patterns 1-4 will be studied in this chapter. Patterns 5 and 6 are deferred to Chapter 14, Section *b*, under the heading, "Syncopation."

a.   *Intervals in the I and V triads :*

305 Animé — France

306 Canon for 5 voices — Praetorius

307 Allegro — Finland

308 Andante   Ohio

309 Con moto   Texas

310 Canon for 3 voices   Beethoven

311 Langsam   Schubert, *Die Leiermann*, Op. 89, No. 24

312 Moderato   Russia

313 Slow   Mexico

314 Allegro non troppo   Italy

315 Allegro   Russia

316 Andantino   Italy

b. Intervals in the V⁷ chord :

317

Allegretto

Germany

Canon for 3 voices

Salieri (1759–1825)

318

326 Vigorously · · · Finland

c. *Intervals in the IV triad:*

327 Lively · · · Germany

328 Moderato · · · France

329 Lively · · · France

334 Allegro — France — Fine — D.C. al Fine

335 Canon for 3 voices — J. Hilton (17th century)

336 Con moto — Germany (Brahms) — Fine — D.C.

337 Allegro — Mozart, *The Magic Flute*, K. 620 — cresc. poco a poco

Allegretto

Sweden

12

Melody

intervals in the I, V, V⁷,
and IV chords

Rhythm

compound time — the beat
and its subdivision into six parts

This chapter presents no new problems in intervals. Section *a* includes intervals in the I, V, and V⁷ chords as studied in Chapter 2 and Chapter 4. Section *b* includes intervals in the IV triad as studied in Chapter 7.

New in this chapter is the subdivision of the beat note into six parts; for example, in $\frac{6}{8}$, $\quad$; in $\frac{6}{4}$, $\quad$; in $\frac{6}{16}$, $\quad$. By tying various members of this six-note group, many rhythmic patterns can be formed. Those most commonly used are:

Other groupings will be found in Chapter 14, Section *b*, "Syncopation."

117

a. *Intervals in the I, V, and V⁷ chords:*

339 Andante   England

340 Andante   Scotland

341 Gaily   England

342 Lent   France

118

cresc.

Con moto

England

349 *p*

cresc.

mf

Canon for 3 voices

Wm. Lawes

350

1

2

3

$\dot\jmath = 1$ beat

Swabia

351 *f*

1. **2.**

Fine mf

D.C.

b. **Intervals in the IV triad :**

Canon for 3 voices

Schubert

352

1

2

120

353 Moderato — Germany

354 Slowly — Alabama

355 Con moto — Spain

356 ♩.=92 England

357 Andante Arlberg (1830–1896), Svärmeri

* Interval of an augmented fourth.

358 ♩.=1 beat Costa Rica

13

Melody

other interval problems

Rhythm

simple and compound time

This chapter combines singing of intervals as studied in Chapter 8 with rhythmic problems as studied in the preceding chapters of Part II.

a.   Diatonic intervals :

359   Andantino   Mozart, Divertimento No. 14, K. 270

360   Canon for 2 voices   Germany

366 Larghetto — Scotland

367 Teneramente — Stephen Foster, *The Village Maiden*

368 Moderato — Argentina

369 Andante   Sweden

Fine

D.C.

370 Lightly   England

371 Allegretto   Grieg, *Lauf der Welt*

126

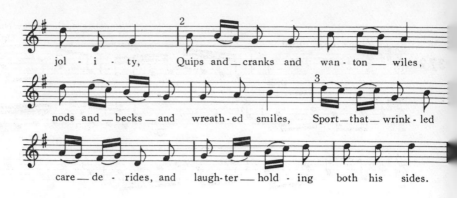

jol - i - ty, Quips and — cranks and wan - ton — wiles,

nods and — becks — and wreath - ed smiles, Sport — that — wrink - led

care — de - rides, and laugh - ter — hold - ing both his sides.

376 Allegro

Telemann, *Tafel Musik*

377 Allegro appassionato

Mendelssohn, Trio No. 2, Op. 66

378 Largo sostenuto

Haydn, Quartet, Op. 33, No. 2

379 Con moto   Purcell, *Dioclesian*

mp

* Interval of a diminished fourth.

380 Adagio   Marcello (1686–1739), Cantata,
L'usignolo che il suo duolo

mf

p

cresc.

f

Couperin, *Soeur Monique*

Tendrement sans lenteur

381

p

cresc.

f

Rimsky-Korsakov, *The Snow Maiden*

Adagio

382

dolce

Grieg, *Holberg Suite*, Op. 40

Allegretto

383

pp

fpp

f

fz

Fine fpp

fpp

f

130

D.C.al
Fine

b. Chromatic tones not implying modulation :

384

Con moto

Schubert, *Frühlingstraum*, Op. 89, No 11.

385

Allegretto

Joseph Steffan (1726–1797), *Gold'ne Freiheit*

386

Larghetto

Mozart, Clarinet Quintet, K. 581

387
Moderato

Schubert, *Um Mitternacht*, Op. 88, No. 3

388
Ernst

K. P. E. Bach, *Der Tag des Weltgerichts*

389
Grazioso

Rimsky-Korsakov, *The Snow Maiden*

390
Grave

J. Peri (c. 1600), Orfeo

391 Andante   Mozart, *La Clemenza di Tito*, K. 621

392 Zart, heimlich   Brahms, *Geliebter, wo zaudert*,
Op. 33, No. 13

393 Allegro   Beethoven, Quartet No. 12, Op. 127

14

Melody

no new material

Rhythm

syncopation

Section *a* of this chapter contains examples of syncopation within the divided beat only, as studied in Chapter 9. These review studies of syncopation are found in melodies containing rhythmic problems from the preceding chapters of Part II.

Section *b* introduces syncopation within the subdivided beat. This includes the rhythmic patterns 𝅘𝅥𝅮 𝅘𝅥 . and 𝅘𝅥𝅮𝅘𝅥𝅮 𝅘𝅥 (see Chapter 11, examples 5-6) as well as the problem of tying the weak part of the subdivided beat into a strong beat or strong part of a beat.

a. *Syncopation in the divided beat only, combined with rhythmic problems in the subdivided beat :*

Moderato   Haydn, Quartet No. 25

394

395 Allegro   Muffat (1690–1770), Suite for Harpsichord

396   Spain

397 Allegretto   Mexico

398

Assai agitato ♩.=180   Schumann, Quartet, Op. 41, No. 3

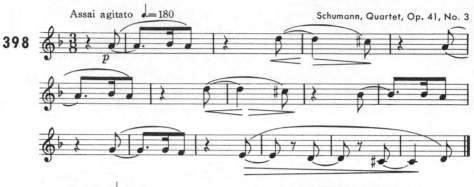

399

Vivace ♩.=86   Dvořák, Quartet, Op. 51

b. Syncopation within the subdivision of the beat:

400

Allegro   South Carolina

401

Andante   Mexico

402 Gaily — Louisiana

403 Allegretto — Scotland

404 Moderato — Florida

137

410 Moderately fast   Negro Spiritual

411 Moderato   Dominican Republic

412 Allegretto   West Indies Calypso*

Bach, Sonata for Flute and
Clavier No. 3

413 Allegro

414 Lento.

Georgia

415 Andante grazioso

Scotland

416

Andantino

Mozart, *Luisita amabile*, K. 480

15

Melody

modulation to closely related keys

Rhythm

simple and compound time

This chapter combines singing modulations as studied in Chapter 10 with rhythmic problems as studied in the preceding chapters of Part II.

419 Largo — Nörmiger's Tablaturbuch (1598)

420 Andante — Arriaga (1822), Quartet No. 2

421 Allegro — Germany

422 Allegro

Schumann, *Der Kartenlegerin*,
Op. 31, No 2

p

rit.

a tempo

423 Andantino

Pasquini (1637–1710), *Quanto è folle*

p

mf

dim.

p

mp

mf

144

428   Allegro   Fauré, Fleur Jetée

429   Andante   Beethoven, *Sehnsucht*, Op. 83, No. 2

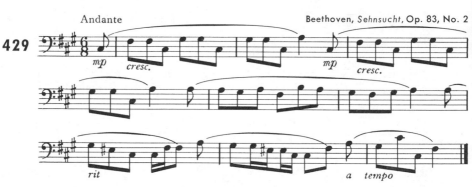

430   Presto   Beethoven, Quartet No. 13, Op. 130

434

Allegro   Schubert, *An den Frühling*

435

Schumann, *Schlusslied des Narren,*
Op. 127, No. 5

Allegro

436 Andantino   Carissimi (1604–1674), *Se dal fonte*

437 Allegretto   Mozart, *Zufriedenheit*

438 Allegro   Mozart, Serenade, K. 388

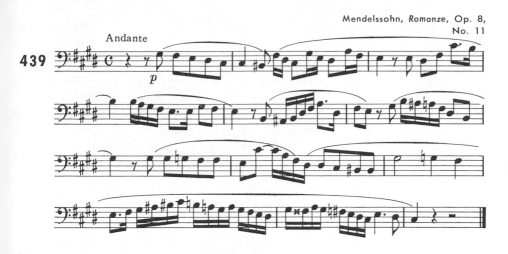

Mendelssohn, *Romanze*, Op. 8, No. 11

Andante

439

Canon for 2 voices
Allegro moderato

Cherubini

440

151

Mozart, *Ridente la calma*, K. 152

441

A. Scarlatti, *Io dissi**

442 Lento

443 Tenderly

Schumann, *Schön Blümelein,*
Op. 43, No. 3

444 Larghetto

Mozart, *The Magic Flute,* K. 620

III

MORE

DIFFICULT

MELODIC

AND

RHYTHMIC

PROBLEMS

16

Review of Parts I and II

melodies more difficult but
within the melodic and rhythmic
limitations of Parts I and II

445   Allegro   Caldara, Che dite

Bourée

E. T. Baron*

446

* From G. P. Telemann, *Der getreue Musikmeister.*

Bach, Brandenburg Concerto, No. 6

447 Allegro

J. C. Bach, Cavatina

448 Larghetto

Berlioz, *The Damnation of Faust,*
Op. 24

449

Allegro ben moderato
Meyerbeer, L'Africaine

450

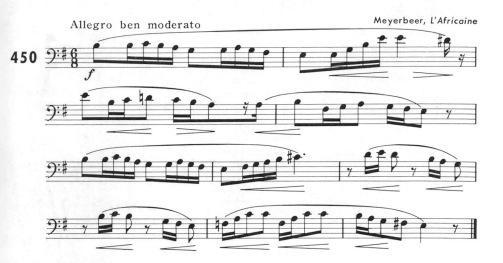

Brahms, *Von ewiger liebe,*
Op. 43, No. 1

Langsam

451

un poco animato

un poco animato   cresc.

f

Andante quasi allegretto   Fauré, Au bord de l'eau

452

p dolce

p

mf

Canon for 6 voices   Beethoven

453

1.

2.

454 Canon for 3 voices — Couperin

455 Canon for 3 voices — Caldara

456

Allegro   *mf*

Handel, *Semele*

Each sa-cred min-strel tunes his lyre, and all in cho-rus.

join   and all

in cho-rus join,   and all   in   cho-rus

sa-cred min-strel tunes his lyre, and   all   in cho-rus join

join   and all,   and   all in cho - rus

and all,   and all,   and all, in cho - rus

and all   in cho-rus join

and all   and all   and all

Adagio

and all,   and all,   in

and all,   and all,   in

cho - rus   join,   in cho - rus   join.

cho - rus   join,   in cho - rus   join.

Moderato   Bach, Cantata No. 125

457

Through-out   the whole earth's broad   ex - panse a   mys - tic

Through - out   the   whole world's broad   ex -

light

panse a   mys - tic   light

is glow-ing.   Through-out   the

is glow-ing.   Through-out   the whole earth's broad   ex -

whole earth's broad ex-panse a mys - tic light

panse a mys - tic light

is glow - ing through-

is glow - ing,

out the earth's ex - panse, through - out the earth's ex -

through - out the earth's ex - panse, the earth's ex -

panse, the earth's ex - panse, the earth's ex - panse, the

panse, the earth's ex - panse. A mys - tic light is

light is ev-er glow - ing.

ev - - er glow - ing. Through-out the

Through - out the whole earth's broad ex-panse a mys - tic

whole world's broad ex - panse a mys - tic light

170

ev - - er glow - ing.

light is ev-er glow - ing. *Fine*

There ech-oes ring-ing far

There ech-oes ring-ing far and

and near, there ech-oes ring-ing far and near, there ech-oes

near, there ech-oes ring-ing. far and near, there ech-oes ring-ing

ring-ing far and near, the word of hope, the

far and near, the word of hope, the word of

word of hope and joy and cheer. Be -

hope and joy and cheer. Be -

liev - ers shall not, per -

liev - ers shall not, per -

* See Part III, Chapter 21, for use of ♩♪ .

ish.   Be - liev-ers   shall   not, shall

ish, be - liev-ers shall   not,   shall

not per - ish.

not per - ish.   *Da capo*

17

Modal Melodies

The modes used in this chapter are those known variously as the *church modes*, the *ecclesiastical modes*, or the *medieval modes*. These modes are :

Mode	White-note scale on keyboard	Characteristic	Example
Aeolian	A	Same as natural (pure) minor	464
Ionian	C	Same as major	
Dorian	D	Similar to natural minor but with a raised sixth scale step	465
Phrygian	E	Similar to natural minor with a lowered second scale step	468
Lydian	F	Similar to major with a raised fourth scale step	469
Mixolydian	G	Similar to major with a lowered seventh scale step	467

As can be seen in the above table, the Dorian mode, for instance, can be found by playing on the piano an ascending scale consisting of white keys only, starting on D. This results in a scale whose pattern of steps and half-steps differs from the patterns of the well-known major and minor scales. This Dorian scale sounds somewhat like a minor scale but differs from D minor in that the sixth scale step is B♮ rather than B♭. The Dorian mode on D could, therefore, have a signature of no sharps and no flats, although it is sometimes found with a signature of one flat (D minor) with B♮ occurring throughout the composition.

Modes can be transposed to begin on any pitch or letter name. To transpose the Dorian mode to G, for example, note that the minor mode on G has two flats; raising the sixth scale step cancels the E♭, leaving one flat (B♭) in the scale.

A modal melody can be found with one or more scale steps not used, making positive identification of the mode impossible. A melody with the tonic note D, using the pitches D E F G A—C D, could be Dorian with B missing or transposed Aeolian with B♭ missing (see melody 472, tonic F).

A modal melody may include altered tones that are not part of the modal scale, for example, the neighboring note G♯ in measure 8 of melody 470.

Use of the modes is very common in folk music all over the world. Up to the time of Bach, the modes listed above were the basis of all musical composition. During the eighteenth and nineteenth centuries, the modes were almost entirely neglected by serious composers. However, twentieth-century composers are using these modes quite extensively.

465 Moderato   Germany

466 Allegro   Massachusetts

467 Con moto   Massachusetts

468 Allegretto   Anon. (13th century)

469 Tempo giusto   Hungary (Bartók)

470 Allegretto   Andalusia

177

471   Moderato   Alec Rowley, *O Lovely Babe*

472   Andante   Scotland

473   Andante   Pennsylvania

474 Andante — England (c. 1460)

475 Canon for 4 voices — Billings

When Je - sus wept. the fall - ing

tear in mer - cy flowd be - yond all bound. When

Je - sus groan'd, a trem - bling fear seiz'd

all ye guilt - y world a - round.

476 Brightly — Illinois

477 Moderato — Ravel, Chanson de la mariée

478 Lento — Spain

479 Alla marcia — France

480 Canon for 3 voices   England

Heigh-ho!   An-y bod-y home?   Food nor drink nor mon-ey have we none,   Yet we shall be mer - - ry.

481 Adagio   Scotland
mf

f

Fine

D.C. al Fine

Heinrich Finck (1542),
O Quam Sanctus Panis Iste

482
p

Arnold von Bruck (1544),
Mitten wir im leben sind

483

Josquin des Prés, *Benedictus*

484

18

Triplet Division
of Undotted-Note Values

Duplet Division
of Dotted-Note Values

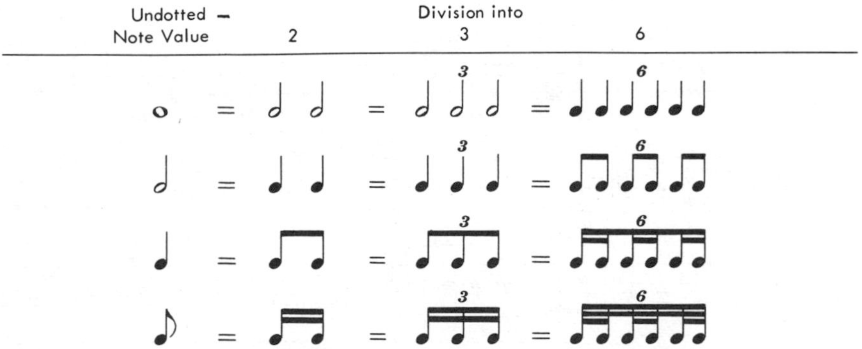

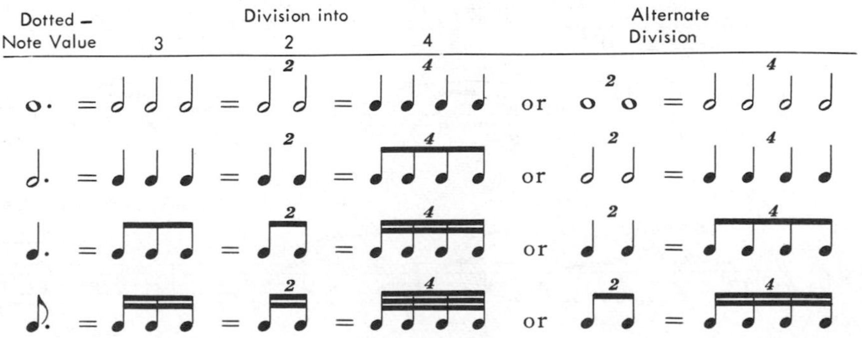

Undotted — Note Value	2	Division into 3	6

Dotted — Note Value	3	Division into 2	4		Alternate Division

As shown above, the same note values are used when dividing any given note value into two or three parts. A few composers use the alternate notation for division of dotted note values as shown in melodies 503, 522, and 608.

Groups of triplets or duplets are often combined, for example,

♩. ♩. = ♪♪ ♪♪ = ♪♪♪♪ , as shown in melody 504.

Dotted-note values are sometimes divided by the next smaller dotted-note values, for example, ♩. = ♪. ♪. = ♪. ♪. ♪. ♪. , as shown in melody 521.

485 Con spirito ... Arizona

486 Con moto ... Mendelssohn, O for the Wings of a Dove

Schumann, *Frühlingsbotschaft*,
Op. 79, No. 3

487

Schnell

Schubert, *Wasserflut*, Op. 89,
No. 6

488

Langsam

488 *(stark)*

489 Moderato   Schubert, *Am Strome*, Op. 8 No. 4

490 Allegro   Händel, *Samson*

188

491

Gaily

Colin Muset (13th century), *Lai*

492 Langsam — Cornelius, *Lied des Narren*

a tempo

poco rit. — *a tempo*

p

f — *p* — *pp*

493 Grave — Brahms, Quintet, Op. 88

p cresc.

p

494 Sostenuto — Giordano, *Fedora*

f

495 Slowly — California

496 Allegro — Spain

497 Moderato   Utah

498 Allegro   Grieg, Das Dichters Gesang

499 Assez animé   France

500 Modéré et gracieux — France

501 Moderato — Pennsylvania

502 Texas

Brückler (1845–1871), *Als ich zum erstenmal dich sah*

503 Herzlich

Franz, Genesung

504 Allegro

poco rit.

Allegro appassionato

Grieg, To Spring

505

fz   rit.   p   a tempo

rit.   f

506 Lento   Spain

mf

mp

507 Andantino   Franz, Liebchen ist da!

p

p   pp

p   p

508 Andante   Portugal

p

509 Langsam   Portugal

510 With breadth and vigor   Byrd, *Make Ye Joy to the World*

Make ye joy to God, all   the   earth, all

the earth.   Make ye joy to God, all the earth, the

earth.   Make ye joy to God, all   the   earth, all   the

earth, serve ye our Lord in glad - ness

Serve ye our Lord in glad - ness. Serve ye our

Lord in glad - ness, in glad - ness.

511 Allegro   Alabama

512 Allegro   England

513 Andante   Spain

514 Moderato   Negro Spiritual

515 Allegretto

Schumann, Faust, Op. 148

sempre p

sempre p

516 Allegro assai

Berlioz, Les Troyens à Carthage

ff

517 Slowly   Negro Spiritual

518 Andante   Binchois (c. 1400–1460), *Misse Angelorum*

Et in spir - i - tum   sanc - tum Do - mi -

Et in spir - i - tum   sanc - tum Do - mi -

num   et vi - vi - fi -

num   et vi -

can - tem   qui ex - pa - tre

vi - fi - can - tem   qui ex pa -

fi - li - o - que   pro - ce - dit.

tre fi - li - o - que pro - ce - dit.

519 Schumann, *Der schwere Abend,*
Op. 90, No. 6

520 Adagio — Slovakia

521 Allegro semplicemente — De Falla, *El Retalbo de Maese Pedro*

522 Allegro — Spain

19

Changing Time Signatures

Less Common Time Signatures

Changing time signatures are usually indicated in one of three ways:

1. The new signature is written at the beginning of the measure in which it occurs. See melody 523.

2. All the time signatures to be used during the composition are placed together at the beginning of the composition. It is necessary to look ahead to determine the meter of each measure. See melody 536.

3. No time signature is given. The meter of each measure must be determined separately. This procedure is often used in transcribing un-barred vocal music of the sixteenth century and earlier. The musical accent coincides with the accentuation of the poetic text. See melody 544.

When music is read from one simple meter to another (e. g., from $\frac{2}{4}$ to $\frac{3}{4}$) or from one compound meter to another (e. g., from $\frac{6}{8}$ to $\frac{9}{8}$), the time value of the beat note is kept constant unless otherwise indicated When the meter changes from simple to compound or vice versa, the length of the divided beat is kept constant unless otherwise indicated:

$\downarrow . = \downarrow$ means: dotted quarter (of following) equals in time value the quarter (of preceding). A number of contemporary composers, however, use this indication with the notation reversed (e. g., in the above illustration, placing $\quad \downarrow = \downarrow .$ over the $\frac{6}{8}$ measure).

Of the less common time signatures, those with 5 and 7 in the numerator are by far the most frequently used. Any number, however, can appear as the numerator of a time signature.

Changing time signatures and the less common signatures have three main uses:

1. The notation of folk music, which very often cannot be written in successive measures of equal length in the common meters.

2. The modern notation of music of the sixteenth century and earlier, which like folk music is often characterized by a lack of regularly recurring measure lengths.

3. The notation of contemporary music. Musical composition in the eighteenth and nineteenth centuries utilized almost exclusively the common time signatures and regularly recurring accent and measure length. Twentieth-century composition, however, uses both the changing meter and the less common meter to a great extent.

526 Lento   Spain

527 Con spirito   Mexico

528 Allegro   France

529 Allegro   ♩=♩. Jamaica

530 France

531 Andante Ohio

532 Allegro molto Spain

533 Texas

534 Tempo giusto   Hungary (Bartók)

535 Langsamer   Schumann, *Jemand*, Op. 25, No. 4

536   Allegro   Czechoslovakia

537   Con moto   Brahms, *Agnes*, Op. 59, No. 5

538   Canon for 3 voices   Byrd

Hey   ho!   to the   Green - wood now let us

go. Sing   heave   and   ho.   And there will we

find both buck and   doe. Sing heave and   ho.   The hart and

hind and the lit - tle pret - ty   roe Sing heave and   ho.

* Canon may end at this point.

539 Molto lento e sostenuto De Falla, *El Retablo de Maese Pedro*

Fine

D.C.

540 Rather fast
1st voice Byrd, *Who Made Thee, Hob*

1. Who made thee, Hob, for - sake the plow and
2. What is her name who bears thy heart with -

2nd voice

1. fall in love? Sweet beau - ty which hath power to bow the
2. in her breast? Syl - va - na fair, of high de - sert, whom

1st voice

1. Gods a - bove What! dost thou serve a shep - herd - ess?
2. I love best. O Hob, I fear she looks too high,

2nd voice

1.
Ay such as hath no peer I guess
2.
Yet love I must or else I die.

Oh Hob. I fear she looks too high, Yet love I must

Yet love I must

or else I die, I die, or else I die, I die.

or else I die, I die, or else I die, I die.

541

542 Tempo giusto   Hungary (Bartók)

543 Largo   Tallis (1567), Why Fumeth in Sight?*

(Melody in Tenor) Why fumeth in sight the Gen - tiles

spite: in fu - ry rag - ing stout. Why

tak'th in hand the peo - ple fond, vain

things to bring a - bout. The kings a -

* This melody is used by Ralph Vaughan Williams in his "Fantasia on a Theme of Thomas Talliis."

210

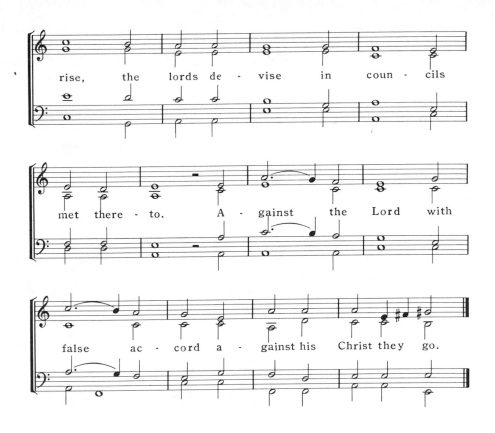

rise, the lords de - vise in coun - cils

met there - to. A - gainst the Lord with

false ac - cord a - gainst his Christ they go.

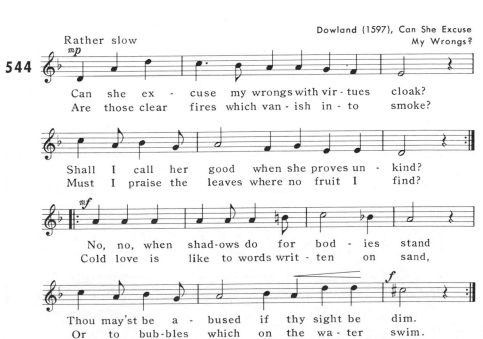

Dowland (1597), Can She Excuse
My Wrongs?

Rather slow

544

Can she ex - cuse my wrongs with vir - tues cloak?
Are those clear fires which van - ish in - to smoke?

Shall I call her good when she proves un - kind?
Must I praise the leaves where no fruit I find?

No, no, when shad - ows do for bod - ies stand
Cold love is like to words writ - ten on sand,

Thou may'st be a - bused if thy sight be dim.
Or to bub - bles which on the wa - ter swim.

Wilt thou be thus a - bus - ed still, see - ing that she will

right thee ne - ver? If thou can'st not o'er - come her

Will thy love will be thus fruit - less ev - er.

545 Allegro   Czechoslovakia

546 Largo   Ireland

547 Andantino   Spain

552 Molto moderato

Elgar, Caractacus

O my war-ri-ors tell me tru-ly o'er the red graves where ye lie. That your mon-arch led you du-ly, first to charge and last to fly. O my war - ri - ors!

553 Moderato

Mexico

554 Pas vite

France

555 Maestoso — Rimsky-Korsakov, *The Snow Maiden*

556 Andantino (♩ = 84) — Moussorgsky, *Boris Gudonov*

557 ♩ = 92 — Maine

558 Allegro
Refrain (repeat refrain after each numbered section)

Mexico

559 Adagio

Spain

20

Further Subdivision of the Beat

The Divided Conductor's Beat

The use of the beat note divided even more than in previous chapters is not common in easier melodic lines. This chapter presents two uses of this notation:

1. The beat note divided into eight parts in simple time:

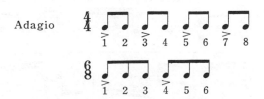

2. The divided conductor's beat: When the tempo of a composition is very slow, often the time signature does not actually express the number of beats in the measure. Thus, in a very slow $\frac{4}{4}$ measure, there will actually be eight beats, the eighth note receiving one beat. In a very slow compound meter, the numerator of the time signature actually indicates the number of beats in the measure. Thus, in a slow $\frac{6}{8}$, instead of two ♩. beats in one measure, there will be six ♪ beats in one measure:

In these slow tempi, it is common to find the use of further subdivision. Thus, in an *adagio* $\frac{2}{4}$, the group of four thirty-second notes will actually represent the beat divided into four parts:

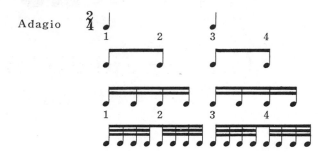

Examples of the divided conductor's beat begin with melody 569.

Because these rhythmic problems are most often identified with difficult melodic lines, many more of these examples will be found in Chapter 22.

563 Andante

564 Andante

565 Adagio

566 Moderato

Haydn, Quartet No. 29

567 Andante

Spohr, Double Quartet, Op. 87

568

Andante

France

p

mp

p

mf

mp

mf

mp

mf

f

mp

cresc.

569 Andante cantabile (♪ = 80)   Donizetti, *Don Pasquale*

570 Andante larghetto   Händel, *Judas Maccabeus*

571

Largo (♪= 72)

Händel, *Athalia*

p dolce

cresc.

mp

mp

224

rit.

Marcello, _Lontananza e gelosia_

572 Adagio (♪=72)

_p_

poco rit.

Schubert, Symphony No. 5

573 Andante con moto

_p_

Haydn, _The Creation_

574 Andante

_p_

cresc.

Sostenuto (♪ = 72)

Piccini, *La buona Figliuola*

575

mp

mf

f

mf

mp

cresc.

f

mf

rit. - - - - - -

21

Remote Modulation

A modulation to any key other than a closely related key is a remote modulation. In practicing remote modulations one should follow the instructions already given for modulation in Part I, Chapter 10, and in Part II, Chapter 15.

576   Langsam   Schubert, *Wehmut* Op. 22, No. 2

577   Langsam   Schubert, *Spät schon, wenn schon längst*

Mendelssohn, *Keine von der Erde
schönen*, Op. Post.

578

Schubert, *Jüngling am Bache*,
Op. 87, No. 3

579

580 Andante poco mosso

Offenbach, *Tales of Hoffman*

581 Andante con moto

Berlioz, The Damnation of Faust

582 Allegro

Berlioz, The Damnation of Faust

583 Moderato

Mahler, *Rhine Legend**

rit.   a tempo

rit.   a tempo

* Copyright 1914 by Universal Edition, Vienna. Copyright renewed 1941 by Alma Mahler-Werfel.

poco rit.   molto rit.   a tempo

riten.   a tempo

Moderately fast   Cornelius, *Verratene Liebe*

584

Schumann, *Ländliches, Lied,*
Op. 29, No. 1

Einfach, fröhlich

585

Meyerbeer, *Dinorah*

Andante

586

martellato

martellato

f

p

f

p

22

Complex Rhythmic Problems Combined with Difficult Melodic Lines

Metheus de Perusio (14th century),
Le greygnour bien

587

588 Andante — Couperin, *Brunette*

589 Allegro (♩=1 beat) J. C. Bach, Vauxhall Song

poco a poco cresc.

f

p

poco a poco cresc.

Handel, Solo Cantata No. 49

590

Handel, *Semele*

591

Bach, Cantata No. 11

592

Bach, Cantata No. 2

593 Moderato

Fine

D.C. al Fine

246

594
Adagio (♪ = 76) Bach, Cantata No. 35

247

D.C. al Fine

595 Langsam

K. P. E. Bach, *Am Kommunionstage*

596 Andante maestoso

Rossini, *The Barber of Seville*

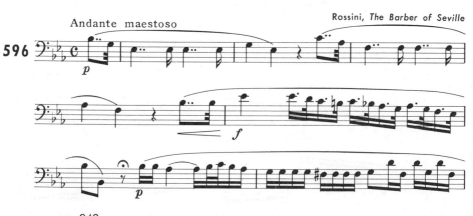

Andante sostenuto

Rossini, *L'Assedio di Corinto*

597

249

Brahms, *Klänge*, Op. 66, No. 1

598

Andante *p*

From the earth the flow'rs are grow - ing, light from

out the sun a - loft, love from out the heart is

flow - - ing, love and pain that

flow - - ing, love and

breaks it oft. Flow'rs to

dust and ash are turn - ing, dark-ness fol - lows af - ter

Flow'rs to dust and ash are turn - ing dark-ness fol - lows

day, love is filled with grief and yearn - -

af - ter day, love is filled with grief and yearn -

ing, grief that wastes sad hearts a-way, griev -

ing, grief that wastes sad hearts a -

ing hearts that waste a - way.

way, griev - ing hearts that waste a - way.

Brahms, *Nachtigall*, Op. 97, No.1

Langsam

599

252

Liszt, Die drei Zigeuner

600

Lento

Allegro vivace

Un poco più lento

Lustig

Mahler, *Scheiden und meiden*

601

602

Hugo Wolf, Der Freund

603 Andante molto mosso

Mascagni, Guglielmo Ratcliff

605 Molto allegro   R. Strauss, *Elektra*

606 Allegro moderato (♩ = 84)   Fauré, *Mandoline*

dimin. p p sempre

p

3

dimin.

pp poco rit. a tempo

Debussy, Mandoline

607

Allegretto

pp

p dim.

pp

mf

608 Flowing
Hindemith, *Das Marienleben*, Op. 27*

Acknowledgments

The author expresses his appreciation to the following individuals and publishers for the use of melodies from their publications:

Victor Bator, Trustee of the Bartók estate: melodies 32, 246, 469, and 542 from *Hungarian Folk Music*, by Béla Bartók, published by Oxford University Press, Inc., New York, N.Y.

Mary O. Eddy, author of *Ballads and Songs from Ohio*, published by J.J. Augustin, Locust Valley, N.Y: melodies 35, 118, 308, and 531.

American Book Company, New York, N.Y.: melody 491 from *Singing Through the Ages*, by Roy Harris and Jacob Evanson; copyright 1940 by American Book Company.

American Folklore Society, Philadelphia, Pa.: melodies 30, 94, 464, 467, 473, and 546 from the *Journal of American Folklore*; melodies 127, 233, 368, 432, and 495 from *Spanish-American Folk Songs*, by Eleanor Hague.

Ascherberg, Hopwood and Crew, Ltd., London: melodies 60, 200, and 228 from *Folk Songs of the North Countrie*, by Frank Kidson; melody 180 from *A Garland of English Folk Songs* by Frank Kidson.

Associated Music Publishers, Inc., New York, N.Y., melody 224 from *Let's Build a Town*, by Paul Hindemith, © Copyright 1931, Schott and Co., Ltd. Used by permission of the publisher and Associated Music Publishers, Inc., agents for the United States of America; melody 608 from *Das Marienleben*, by Paul Hindemith, © Copyright 1923, Schott & Co. Ltd, used by permission of Associated Music Publishers, Inc., agents for the United States of America; melodies 5, 15, 22, 27, 52, 55, 75, 90, 125, 315, 316, and 551 from *Das Lied der Volker*, by Heinrich Möller, © Copyright 1929, 1956 by B. Schott's Soehne, Mainz, used by permission of copyright, owner and its agent, Associated Music Publishers, Inc.; melodies 314, 536, and 545 from *Folk Dance Music of the Slavic Nations*, by H.A. Schimmerling, © Copyright 1951 by Associated Music Publishers, Inc.

Boosey and Hawkes, Inc., New York, N.Y.: melody 605 from *Elektra*, by Richard Strauss.

C.F. Peters Corporation, New York, N.Y.: melodies 447 and 589 from *12 Konzert und Opern Arien*, by J.C. Bach, copyright C.F. Peters Corporation, 373 Park Avenue South, New York, N.Y. 10016, reprinted with permission of the publishers; melodies 388 and 595 from *30 Geistliche Lieder*, by C.P.E. Bach, copyright C.F. Peters Corporation, reprinted with permission; melodies 423 and 436 from *Alte Meister des Bel Canto*, copyright C.F. Peters Corporation, reprinted with permission; melodies 3, 7, 17, 91, 104, 170, 173, 174, and 274 from *Deutschland im Volkslied,* by Gustav Kniep, copyright C. F. Peters Corporation, reprinted with permission.

Carl Fischer, Inc., New York, N. Y. melody 518 from *Documenta Polyphonae Liturgicae S. Ecclesiae Romanae,* copyright by Societas Universalis Sanctae Ceciliae, Rome 1949, Carl Fischer, Inc., New York, N. Y., sole selling agents, reprinted by permission.

Columbia University Press, New York, N. Y.: melody 68 from *A Song Catcher in the Southern Mountains,* by Dorothy Scarborough, page 402, " The Wexford Girl."

Duke University Press, Durham, N. C.: melody 460 from *The Frank C. Brown Collection of North Carolina Folklore,* Volume 5.

Elkan-Vogel Co., melody 607 from *Douze Chants,* by Claude Debussy, Durand et Cie of Paris, copyright owners, Elkan-Vogel Company, Philadelphia, sole agents; melody 477 from *Cinq Melodies Populaires Grecques,* by Maurice Ravel, Durand et Cie of Paris, copyright owners, Elkan-Vogel Company, Philadelphia, sole agents.

G. Schirmer, Inc., New York, N. Y.: melody 257 from *Anthology of Italian Song,* by A. Parisotti; melodies 129, 138, 199, and 230 from *44 French Folk Songs and Variants,* by Julien Tiersot; melody 95 from *Reliquary of English Song;* melodies 59, 83, and 242 from *Songs of Italy,* by E. Marzo; melodies 338 and 369 from *Songs of Sweden,* by Gustaf Hagg.

Gesellschaft zur Herausgabe von Denkmälern der Tonkunst in Österreich, Vienna : melodies 385 and 445 from *Denkmäler der Tonkunst in Öster-reich.*

Harvard University Press, Cambridge, Mass.: melodies 395 and 541 reprinted by permission of the publishers from Willi Apel and Archibald T. Davison, *Historical Anthology of Music,* Vol. I and II. Copyright 1946, 1949, 1950 by the President and Fellows of Harvard College.

Hispanic Institute, New York, N. Y.: melodies 8, 20, 29, 245, 355, 478, 506, 508, 509, 513, 532, and 559 from *Folk Music and Poetry of Spain and Portugal,* by Kurt Schindler. Courtesy of Hispanic Institute, Columbia University.

H. W. Gray Company, New York, N. Y.: melodies 44, 76, 132, 177, 187, 349, and 512 from *Folk Songs, Chanteys and Singing Games,* by Charles Farnsworth and Cecil Sharp reprinted by permission of Novello & Co., Ltd.; melody 362 from *Folk Songs from Mexico and South America,* by Eleanor Hague.

Indiana University Press, Bloomington, Ind.: melody 75 from *Ballads and Songs of Indiana,* edited by Paul G. Brewster.

International Music Company, New York, N. Y.: melody 601, *Scheiden und Meiden,* by Gustav Mahler.

J. and W. Chester, Ltd., London : melodies 375 and 419 from *El Retablo de Maese Pedro*, by Manuel de Falla, printed by permission of the owners of copyright, J. and W. Chester, Ltd., 11, Gt. Marlborough Street, London, W. 1.

Josef Weinberger, Ltd., London: melody 133 from *The Jewels of the Madonna*, by Ermano Wolf-Ferrari, copyright Josef Weinberger, Ltd., London; U. S. A. copyright renewed 1961 by Josef Weinberger, Ltd., London.

Libraire Renouard, Paris: melody 168 from *La Musique des Troubadours*, by Jean Beck, H. Laurens, éditeur, Paris.

Louisiana State University Press, Baton Rouge: melodies 85, 95, 221, and 402 from *Louisiana-French Folk Songs*, by Irene Whitfield.

M. Baron Company, Oyster Bay, Long Island, New York: melody 412 from *Calypso Songs*, by Massie Patterson and Lionel Belasco; copyright 1943 by M. Baron Co.

Mediaeval Academy of America, Cambridge, Mass.: melody 587 from *French Secular Music of the 14th Century*, by Willi Apel.

Novello & Company, Ltd., London: melody 552 from *Caractacus*, by Sir Edward Elgar; reproduced by permission of Novello & Co., Ltd., London; melody 471 from *O Lovely Babe*, by Alec Rowley, reproduced by permission of Novello & Co., Ltd., London.

Oxford University Press, Inc., London: melody 14 from *Folk Songs from the Southern Appalachians*, by Cecil Sharp.

Stainer & Bell Ltd., Surrey, England: melody 212, "Never Weather-Beaten Sail," by Thomas Campion; melody 544, "Can She Excuse My Wrongs?" by John Dowland; melodies 510 and 540 from *The Collected Works of Willam Byrd*.

Theodore Presser Company, Bryn Mawr, Pa.: melody 433 from *One Hundred Folk Songs of All Nations*, by Granville Bantock, copyright 1911 by Oliver Ditson, used by permission; melodies 63, 124, 126, and 140 from *Sixty Folk Songs of France*, by Julien Tiersot, copyright 1915 by Oliver Ditson, used by permission.

University of Alabama Press, University, Alabama: melodies 193, 254, 332, 354, 405, and 511 from *Folk Songs of Alabama*, by Byron Arnold.

University of Arizona Press, Tuscon: melodies 258, 261, and 485 from *Canciones de Mi Padre* (Vol. XVII, No. 1), by Luisa Espinel, by permission of the University of Arizona Press.

University of Utah Press, Salt Lake City: melody 497 from *Ballads and Songs From Utah*, by Lester A. Hubbard, University of Utah Press, 1961.

Vermont Printing Company, Brattleboro: melodies 122, 256, 396, and 547 from *Cancionero Espanol*, by Maria Diez de Oñate.

Yale University Press, New Haven, Conn.: melody 557 from *British Ballads From Maine*, by Phillips Barry.